To Jessie –

Mandy Harn

Act Like You've Got Some *Sense*

Collected works of

Mandy Flynn

authorHOUSE

1663 LIBERTY DRIVE, SUITE 200
BLOOMINGTON, INDIANA 47403
(800) 839-8640
www.authorhouse.com

First published by AuthorHouse 06/07/04

ISBN: 1-4184-4043-4 (e)
ISBN: 1-4184-4042-6 (sc)

Library of Congress Control Number: 2004093386

Printed in the United States of America
Bloomington, Indiana

This book is printed on acid-free paper.

To

Mike, Trey & Carter

3 Squeezes

Table of Contents

Act Like You've Got Some Sense

I stood there watching as my son boarded a big chartered bus, his blue backpack slung over one shoulder and a pillow crunched under the other arm. He turned to smile at me before disappearing amid the mass of other fourth grade boys already on board and ready to set out on a church trip to Sea World.

I looked around. A dozen or so other mothers and a good number of dads stood waiting in the church parking lot. It was chilly. My nose was cold.

"You can stand over there and look sad as the bus pulls away," my son had suggested after we'd packed his sleeping bag away under the bus. He knows me too well. I tend to hover.

"Have fun," I then said, wrapping him in a big hug. "Stay with the group," I pleaded as he let out a desperate sigh. "I love you," I assured him as he peeled my arms from their death grip around

1

his neck. I think he was afraid I'd start singing "You Are The Wind Beneath My Wings" if he didn't get away in a hurry.

It's been known to happen.

"I'll be fine," he said and turned to climb the steps to the bus. I'd forgotten something – six of the most important words a mother can tell her child.

"Act like you've got some sense," I yelled.

No response. Did he hear me? I wasn't sure.

That's OK. He's heard it almost every day of his young life, I told myself. Surely, it's sunk in by now.

Act like you've got some sense. It was a standard around our house growing up. As commonplace as brush your teeth, feed the dog and stop aggravating your sister.

"Act like you've got some sense," they'd tell us.

We never really talked about people. All someone had to say was, "That boy doesn't have any sense," and we all knew what they meant. Usually, not having any sense meant you'd done something stupid. "That boy ain't right," was worse. You usually can get some sense, but if you ain't right, then you just ain't right.

What was worse, too, than not having any sense was acting like you didn't have any home schoolin'. That usually meant you didn't say "Yes, ma'm" or "Thank you" to the grown ups.

Acting like you didn't have home schoolin' was bad because it reflected on your mama. And if mama found out you acted like she didn't raise you right, well then you were really in trouble.

These morsels of social etiquette became increasingly clearer when I became a mother, myself. I can sense an absent ma'm from the lips of my child from 50 yards away and cringe at a forgotten thank you. We're not perfect, but we're working on it.

Almost every day, it's the same drill. Most mornings, they tune me out. The other day, my daughter was listening.

"Have a good day," I told her as she got out of the car to go into school. "I love you," I said as she put her pink book bag on her shoulder. "Act like you've got some sense," I threw in for good measure.

She scratched her nose.

"Yes, ma'm," she said. "I do. In my piggy bank up in my room." Then she skipped on up the sidewalk and into first grade.

Oh, well. I guess it's always good to have that kind, too.

I blinked

I blinked.

I blinked and summer's nearly gone.

Oh, the days are still warm. Sticky hot. Where paper thin layers of cool sweat blanket your arms and trickles creep down the back of your t-shirt. Mosquitoes munch on ankles and uncovered knees. Late afternoon thunder chases away the chance for a game of catch.

Fuzzy peaches still wait beside the window sill. Fresh tomatoes slice up rich and red and cool in the refrigerator. Books and pencils cleared from the table make room for plates. Maybe there's time for a swim after supper's done. Just maybe.

I blinked and summer's nearly gone.

Like summers of another time when we would breathe in every second of a pretty day, making playhouses in the dirt until dusk, hosing off our bare feet by the back porch. Waiting to help daddy pull off his boots. Grab the heel. The smells of country fried steak calling from the kitchen. Iced tea and paper napkins.

Dishes done.

Sometimes we'd walk.

Cool grass on naked toes, but only until the sidewalk started. Just down from our neighbor's house, past the red dirt path and the pomegranates, sweet and sour at the same time. Careful, don't step on a crack. You'll break your mother's back.

Past the white wooden church with its dirt swept yard and rainbow windows. Where little wooden chairs lined up for Sunday School and the big piano sat poised for Miss Carol's magic fingers. Onward Christian Soldiers. No need for a hymnal. We knew the words by heart.

Follow the sidewalk. If only it could talk. Past houses bathed in peace, windows glowing in soft yellow light and wispy curtains, propped up to catch a breeze or voices of walkers passing by.

Screen doors creak open. The universal smalltown hello. Heavy footsteps on the wooden porch, a sigh as someone settles in a rocker. Stop to chat. Sit a spell. My how they've grown. Darkness washes in.

Eyes shut tight. Star bright. Star light. First star I see tonight. Can't tell your wish or it won't come true. Everybody knows that.

5

Bobwhites and frogs sing in tune to the lightening bugs' dance. Tiny beacons in a backdrop of honeysuckle. Catch one if you can, but let it go. Can't we keep just one?

Follow the sidewalk home, past houses where lights are now dimmed, rocking chairs now empty. Sounds of television float through front door screens. Past the church with its towering steeple. Pomegranates dot the ground. The sidewalk ends.

Hands cupped, carrying a precious find. Find me a jar, please, from under the kitchen sink. Rinse it out. Dry it well. Tiny holes poked in the top.

My sister sleeps across the room. A fan whirs in the corner. The moon dribbles through the tall window, across my green bedspread. Underneath the wooden doors, the baseball game crackles softly from my father's radio. A perfect summer night.

And then I blinked. And it was gone.

I listened to the preacher's words on Sunday. My daughter's hand rested in mine, tiny fingers squeezing messages. Three squeezes. I love you, too, I squeezed back.

Don't let time get away from you, the preacher said. Don't be idle. Live.

Because in a blink, the chance is gone. Like summers tend to be.

Maybe tonight we'll walk.

After supper. We won't step on cracks and we'll yearn for a sidewalk to follow. We'll hold hands and squeeze messages and look up at the sky.

Star light. Star bright. First star I see tonight. I wish I may, I wish I might have the wish I wish tonight.

I wish I didn't have to blink.

Quiet Time Is Overrated

My daughter has been singing the same song for the last two hours and twenty four minutes. It may have been longer, but I've closed myself in my room and put a pillow over my head

At first, her singing was adorable. After twenty minutes, it was cute. After an hour... I needed to put a pillow over my head.

Knock. Knock. Knock.

"What are you doin' in there?" she asks me through the closed door.

I'm used to having conversations with my children behind closed doors. Take last night, for instance.

Click. That's the sound of me shutting the bathroom door.

Five. Four. Three. Two. One.

Knock. Knock. Knock.

"What are you doin' in there?" my five-year-old yells. There is water running. I'm about to take a bath.

"I'm taking a bath." I yell back. "I need some quiet time."

Jiggle. Jaggle. That's the sound of her trying to open the locked door. "Why?" she asks.

"Because I want to," I tell her.

"Why?" she asks again.

Silence. Maybe if I ignore her she'll go away.

Jiggle. Jaggle.

"Are you still in there?"

Maybe a diversion will work.

"I think I hear your daddy calling you," I tell her.

Pitter. Patter. She runs away.

Ahhhh. Silence at last....

Pitter. Patter. She's back.

Jiggle. Jaggle. "Daddy said he didn't call me," she says.

Note to self: Advise daddy of the diversion technique.

"Honey, go play until I get out, okay?"

"Oh-kaaaaaaay," she says dramatically. Pitter. Patter.

Five. Four. Three. Two. One.

"Mommy? Can you put Barbie's dress on?"

I look to the door just as a pink and green mini dress appears underneath. This isn't the first time things have appeared under

9

the doorway as I'm trying to take a bath. Books. Notes. M&Ms. I've seen it all.

Tonight, though, I hear a noise I haven't heard before. A tiny crunch.

Half of Barbie's leg has made it under the doorway, but the rest of her is having a spot of trouble. "She won't fit!" my daughter yells. She's mad

I've not raised a child that gives up too easily. There's huffing. There's grumbling. There's a ….Cruunnnnch!

Barbie's whole leg makes it under the doorway. Her body, I am sad to say, does not.

"Her leg! Her leg!" she yells. "Barbie's only got one leg!"

Now the one whose arms the dog chewed off won't feel so awkward, I think to myself. I hear a sob. That's my cue.

I open the door to her holding a naked one-legged Barbie in one hand and rubbing her eyes with the other. I guess I'll have some quiet time another day.

But not today. My daughter has been singing the same song for two hours and twenty five minutes now. And I, being a mother who doesn't want to tell her to stop... but who doesn't want to go crazy, either... have closed myself in my room with a pillow over my head.

Crinkle. Slide.

That's the sound of a note being passed under my closed bedroom door. It's written in crayon.

"Wont tu here me seng?" it says. Too cute. I open the door to her holding a crayon in one hand and a one-legged Barbie in the other.

"Her leg fell off again," she says, handing her doll to me and turning to sing "I Like To Eat Apples and Bananas" for the three hundred and seventy second time as she skips back down the hall.

Quiet time is overrated, I suppose. But maybe not for Barbie. That girl needs all the help she can get.

I Call Shotgun

I had a flashback the other day, and it all started with my husband putting on my daughter's shoes.

No, not on himself. On her. There they sat, the two of them, in the middle of the bedroom floor when from down the hallway came those three words that we've all heard at some point in our lives.

I call shotgun.

You see, the three of them – my husband, my son and my daughter – were going out to lunch and leaving me at home alone. No, you don't have to feel sorry for me. I was happy!

Until I saw the lip. And then heard the moan. That led to the whimper. That opened up the door to the all out pout. My daughter was mad that her brother had called shotgun first.

What's the big deal about where you sit in the truck as long as everybody's safe? I wondered.

Then I did something I've caught myself doing more and more of as the years go by. I quoted my parents.

"It doesn't matter where you sit. You're all going to get there at the same time."

Ouch.

The lip got bigger. I tried to console her. But the whole time I tried to cheer her up I couldn't help but think about my own self some 25 years ago when I wanted desperately nothing more than to sit in some place of honor in the car.

I have five brothers and sisters – four older than myself. For years, I was banished to the back seat on the way to school each day. And one of them drove a Vega.

I don't know if you know what a Vega is, but it's a very small car. I can't recall much about it, myself, because I was always stuck in the tiny back seat where I'd clutch my book bag to my chest and my knees went up my nose. My flashback includes having to listen to "The Night The Lights Went Out In Georgia" over and over on eight track.

Don't feel sorry for me now, either. They'd let me sit in the front on my birthday.

I felt like a queen, as much as a little kid could, sitting next to my cool big brother or sister as we cruised to school. It was an honor.

13

I remember hoping beyond hope that someone would see me get out of the car when I got to school on those days – out of the front seat – and think I was cool, too.

Only, that's another thing about having your teenage sibling drive you to school – they always dropped me off forty five minutes early so they could go be cool in the parking lot with their friends over at the high school.

That said, the only people who got to witness my once-a-year moment of coolness were the janitor and the handful of other pitiful kids like myself whose older brothers and sisters dropped them off too early, too.

So when my daughter got mad the other day because her brother called shot gun, I could relate. Reaching deep into my own experiences, I tried to make her feel better.

"It's really no big deal to get shotgun," I said. "I don't even know what it means, do you?"

She shook her head no. "See?" I offered. "It's no big deal. When I was little I never got to sit up front and, look at me, I'm cool, aren't I?"

She looked at me. She thought about it, she really did. She started to cry again.

So, my daughter doesn't think I'm cool. That's OK. Somewhere, there's a janitor and three weird now grown up kids that saw me get out of that Vega on my birthday twenty five years ago and they think I'm cool.

Now, you may feel sorry for me.

The Things We Say

We were driving down the road the other day when the most incredible thing happened.

My husband turned into my mother. Or was it his father? Or maybe it was his mother. It could have been any of them, actually.

In his defense, he was provoked.

"Don't touch me," said our 6-year-old to her brother.

"You don't touch me," said our 9-year-old to his sister.

"You touched me first," she said.

"You touched me first," he said.

"You," she said.

"You," he said.

"You!" she said.

And then it happened. My husband morphed.

"Do I have to stop this car and get a switch?" he blurted out. He even put his foot on the brake and slowed down for added drama.

Silence. I looked over at him. He looked at me. And then we both burst out laughing.

"Remember that one?" he asked me and I was immediately thrown back to our wood paneled station wagon with my five brothers and sisters.

Oh, yeah. I remember that one. I don't recall a time my parents actually followed through and stopped the car on the side of the road to get a switch. Just the threat was enough to make us shut our mouths and keep our hands to ourselves long enough to get home, or for the next five minutes, whichever came first.

I do remember on occasion wondering where they would find a switch in the middle of town when I didn't see a bush anywhere. But I would never ask such a thing. There were plenty of wide open pastures with lots of bushes on the way home. What's the city folk version of the switch, I wondered?

I had heard, of course, those switch legends about mothers and grandmothers that actually had an official switch that they kept on top of the refrigerator or underneath the front seat of the car. And then there were those really mean ones that made their children go out and pick their own switches off the official switch tree in the back yard.

Those stories put enough fear in me to keep me – and I'm proud to say – switch free during my childhood. Surprisingly, that fear wasn't passed on to my own children.

"What's a switch?" asked our daughter after her father's quite impressive tactic.

Oh, well. At least they stopped fighting, even if the threat was lost. Just add that one to the long list of other things we never thought we'd say as parents. My list keeps getting longer every day.

"Don't make me stop this car.

"Your face is going to freeze like that.

"I'm going to smell you to make sure you really bathed.

"Because I said so.

"Don't sit on your sister's head.

"I don't know where your shoes are. I don't wear your shoes.

"What did you think would happen if you put your finger in the dog's mouth?

"Wipe that look off your face.

"Don't sit so close to the television.

"Are you trying to drive me crazy?

And my personal favorite, "Green beans never killed anybody."

Of course, I often wanted to debate that as a child, as well. Surely, somewhere in the world, someone had died either from eating a poison green bean or from an unfortunate green bean packing accident.

But I'd never ask such a thing. And I went ahead and ate them.

Because I was too short to see on top of the refrigerator.

And you never know what might be up there.

Dancing Queen

It's amazing how much you can find out on a cloudy summer afternoon.

We had just settled in for a nice afternoon of running errands. The dry cleaner. The drug store. The bank.

Aw, shucks. There's a line at the bank drive thru. Things seem to be moving along pretty quickly, though, so we'll just wait our turn, I tell my crew of two in the back seat. I settle back in my seat to wait... turn up the radio... Hmmmm, I like this song.

Click. Thud.

It takes my nine-year-old two seconds flat to unclick his seatbelt and hit the floorboard. Thank goodness we were in park.

"What's wrong with you?!" I yell, thinking he's been stung by a bee or, worse, maimed by his little sister.

"Mom!" he says loudly, but muffled, from his face down position on the floor mat. He drags the word Mom out into three syllables.

"You were...(gasp!)... dancing!"

The horror.

"Dancing?" I ask, puzzled. "Do you mean this?" He peers up at me from his fetal position and I jiggle my right shoulder up and down three times in beat to the music.

"Mom! Stop it! They can see you!"

"Who?"

"Them!" he says, sticking a finger toward the window that he's careful not to let his head rise above for fear someone might see him.

I look around. There are two cars in front of us and one behind. No one's paying attention to me, I assure him. "Now put your belt back on," I tell him.

"Are you gonna dance again?" he asks in a half whisper. He looks worried. I laugh, drive forward a car's length and put the car back in park.

The day has come. I knew it would. My son is embarrassed by me.

I don't recall being embarrassed by my own parents, but I'm sure there were times that I was. My mom never went to the grocery store with curlers in her hair, or wore her bedroom shoes to school that I can remember. My father did, on occasion, wear Bermuda shorts with dark socks, but not so much as to totally devastate my existence as a pre-teen.

I peek in the rear view mirror to make sure my son's securely back in his seat before I turn the radio up once again, careful not to move my arm or shoulder in any semblance that might be construed as a dance move.

Click. Thud.

"Mom!"

"I wasn't jiggling or anything that time, I swear," I say, puzzled. He huffs. I'm afraid now he might get a cramp wedged between the seats like that.

"But you were... (insert another huff here) ... singing!" he breathes, referring to my half hum, half murmur attempt.

"Just so I'll know," I venture, turning down the radio. "What exactly am I allowed to do?" He's back in his seat now, carefully surveying the surroundings to make sure no one's staring at this dancing, singing woman thing that must drive him around.

"Can I tap my thumb on the steering wheel?" I ask.

"OK," he allows. "But not too much."

"Can I tap my foot? No one can see my feet," I ask.

"OK, I guess so," he succumbs.

I drive forward a couple more feet. When did all of this come about, I wonder as I look in my rear view mirror to see my five-year-old boogying in her car seat while her brother shoots her dirty looks. It won't be long until I start embarrassing her, too.

I look over and wave to the woman in the car next to us.

Click. Thud.

What? No waving, either?

It's amazing how much you can find out on a cloudy summer afternoon, sitting in your vehicle in line at the bank. Imagine what possibilities arise when I actually get out of the car. Thank goodness I left my dark socks at home.

Or did I?

Click. Thud.

How Old Do They Think I Am?

What was it like when you were a little girl, they ask me. I pause, sure that I'm too young to be asked such a thing. Shouldn't that question come to little ladies wrapped in the smell of powder and crocheted afghans on their laps?

Impatient with my pause, they ask again. Did you have electricity... were there televisions and telephones?

How old do they think I am?

And so I tell them the story of me as a little girl. It was as close to heaven as I could have imagined at that age, I tell them – that barefoot world of icy orange push-ups and Saturday morning cartoons.

How long it had been since I'd remembered...

My Holly Hobby bedspread. Waking up early to watch Captain Kangaroo and wondering why Bunny Rabbit wore glasses if carrots were supposed to be so good for your eyes. My first crush, I am sure, on Mr. Green Jeans.

Our sweet Johnnie Mae – God rest her soul – how she'd put up with my antics as mama and daddy worked at the peanut warehouse, giving me Tang and Fruit Loops – an occasional cookie for breakfast if I promised not to tell.

The little dirt road near my house, where honeysuckle vines crept through the fence posts and our small hands reached without a scratch under the rusty barbed wire to clutch handfuls of tiny white and yellow honeysuckle flowers. We'd breathe in their sweetness and place the blooms behind our ears to save as the perfect bouquets for our Barbies.

No one worried about strangers or harm or us children riding free on our bikes all the day long. We'd come home when we got hungry or stubbed our toe on the sidewalk – the first true sign that summer had arrived. Mecurichrome or methiolade – which one burned? I always picked the wrong one.

Making mud pies and selling them to daddy for a quarter when he came home from work. Watching The Brady Bunch and Laverne & Shirley on prime time television, thinking Pinkie Tuscadero was rather risqué and being too cool for school with my Fonzie lunch box.

Saturday morning cartoons. Hong Kong Phooey and Grape Ape. Going grocery shopping at the Piggly Wiggly.

"The Piggly what?"

I am old. My own children have never heard of the Piggly Wiggly.

"How old are you?" my daughter asks as I'm brushing her hair before school. It is my birthday and she is more excited about the day than I am, I realize.

"I am 35," I tell her. Lord, I recall when my own parents were 35 – I was just her age. I didn't think they were old... I thought they were ancient!

"Do you think I'm old?" I ask her. She looks thoughtful.

"You're not young," she says.

"No, I'm not young," I say. "But I feel like a teenager."

There's that thoughtful look again.

"You might feel like a teenager," she offers, tugging at her ponytail. "But you don't look like one."

Darn me for giving her that talk about always being honest.

What do I look like, I ask.

"You look like a mommy," she says, hopping down from the stool and bouncing out the bathroom door. How sweet... I think.

Then, from the end of the hallway it came.

"But you do have wrinkles."

Last week – the talk about always being honest.

This week – tact.

Oh, but for the barefoot days of orange push ups and Captain Kangaroo.

Come to think of it, he had wrinkles, too.

I do believe you're as old as you feel.

I feel like a having a cookie for breakfast.

Just another night out

There we are, my husband and I. The two of us. A nice Friday evening, sitting side by side in the restaurant.

I look into his eyes. He looks into mine. A peanut shell flies by my head.

Oh, yeah, our children were there, too.

"Please don't throw the peanut shells," I tell my son as he reaches into the bucket of salty legumes on our table and cracks open another one.

"You're supposed to put them on the floor," he informs me, tossing another shell across the table into the aisle, clearing the steak and potatoes of the man at the next table by only a few inches.

As difficult as it is to get used to the idea of putting peanut shells on the floor, he was right. It is totally acceptable at this restaurant.

That's part of the charm of the place. Only I can't bring myself to put them on the floor so I make a little pile by my tea glass.

"Can we start doing this at home?" he asks, putting a peanut shell on his sister's head. She frowns and swipes it off and he makes another toss over the table.

"Please drop them on the floor, not throw them," I tell him in one of those closed-teeth whispers that's disguised as a smile – a clever move designed to get your point across while not alerting others around you. "And, no. You can't do this at home. Who would clean it up?"

He looks surprised. The horror of me asking such a thing.

"You!" pipes in my daughter and my son shakes his head in agreement. He tosses a shell dangerously close to the table next to us again. I give him the look. It doesn't work.

"Could you tell your son not to throw the peanut shells?" I ask their father.

No answer.

"Help me out here," I appeal to him again, my attention on my neat little pile of peanut shells that I've decided to arrange into the shape of a heart.

Still, no answer.

Oh my Lord, could he be choking on a peanut? I turn to him, ready to save his life.

His eyes are glassed over, but not because he's choking. There's a television hanging nearby and there are sports on. I've lost him.

Alas, it's a condition I've come to accept. I lose him to television several times a year. The entire football season. Some golf tournaments. Baseball games. When there's a game on, I'm used to not being able to tal...

"Shhhh, there's a game on."

Now, it's basketball. I cannot compete.

On occasion, however, I do win. Like when I turn the television to one of those home improvement shows and pretend I can't find the remote. He'll look for ten minutes before he'll walk the extra five feet to turn the channel – gasp! – by hand.

It's a cheap shot, I know. But it's fun. Ice skating and any movie with Barbra Streisand also drive him crazy. I've done research.

But there's no remote to hide in the restaurant.

Our food arrives. We eat without incident until my daughter asks my son what the tartar sauce is and he tells her it's white chocolate. I've told her not to believe everything he says. Should this be one of those learning lessons?

Too late. She spits it out, gives him the meanest look I've ever seen come from a five-year-old, and sticks a napkin to her stuck-out tongue. Her brother wails in laughter as he cracks open another peanut and lobs the shell to the floor.

Just another dinner out with the family.

I look into my husband's eyes. He looks into mine... hey, he's not looking into my eyes.... He's watching the television behind me. Smooth move. I predict we won't be able to find the remote when we get home.

Check please.

My roots are showing

I t's raining again.

It's raining again and the water kicked up from the tires of the blue car in front of me is covering my windshield like a blanket. My wipers squeak as they erase the tiny droplets and grunt as they push their way over a smudge of pine sap smack dab in the center of the windshield.

I can see now. I see that the cars driving toward me all have their lights on, pulling slowly out of the church parking lot up ahead, led by a policeman whose lights are flashing quietly in the rain. A funeral.

I pull over.

The blue car in front of me keeps going. The car behind me honks and passes me by. A gray pick up truck pulls over behind me, followed by a red SUV and a station wagon. Through the mist ahead of me I count four more vehicles pulled silently to the side of the road.

Our roots are showing.

I have groceries in the car. It is six minutes until time to pick my daughter up from ballet class and by the time I get halfway across town I will surely be at least two minutes late, if not more. Miss Peggy won't mind. I'm sure she's shown her roots, too.

A Cadillac drives by and puts on brakes just as it passes, then pulls off onto the muddy roadside in front of me. A car blaring loud music sprays our cars with water as it makes its way past.

The last driver in the somber line pulling from the parking lot makes his way onto the roadway. He passes us by and the line of cars settled on the roadside eases back into traffic. For a minute and a half of a rainy afternoon a handful of strangers have something in common.

Our roots showed. And that's just fine with me.

My roots dig deep. They're twisted and gnarled in the red south Georgia clay that fertilizes my soul. They're not afraid to be out in the open. They don't like to hide. Sometimes they show themselves when I don't even realize it.

My roots make me give up my seat for the older lady standing among us and they don't let me forget to call my mother. They make me cook ham in my black eyed peas and put ice in my sweet tea. They remind my children to say their prayers and wrap them up in the crocheted afghan their great grandmother gave them. They have a strong faith and speak softly. Their heart races at the smell of a turned peanut field. They prefer cornbread dressing over stuffing.

"Where were you?" asks my daughter as we jump over puddles on our way to the car, her legs wrapped around my waist and her body settled on my hip so her tiny pink ballet shoes won't get wet. Her arms are wrapped around my neck. I am three minutes late.

"I had to stop for something," I tell her as I deposit her on the back seat and slide into the front, catching a glimpse of my reflection in the mirror as I pull the damp hair from my collar. I look closer. Darn.

My other roots are showing. These, I'd just as soon hide.

But the others, they'll keep me pulling over.

And that's just fine with me.

The Junk Drawer

It was an ordinary evening at home. I needed a pen.

Maybe there's one in the... (insert Jaws music here)... junk drawer.

Everybody has one. I grew up with one. That one drawer in the house that gathers pens and pencils, sticks of gum, extra appliance parts, owners' manuals, and just about everything else that you don't have a place for.

I needed a pen. I was going in.

I grasped the handle. I pulled. It didn't budge. I pulled again. It squeaked and opened about a quarter of an inch.

My junk drawer floweth over. It was time to clean it out.

After a few hearty tugs and a clever poking around with a spatula handle, I got it open. I stood speechless looking down at what was before me.

Batteries, all shapes and sizes. Were they good or duds? Fishing line. Candles. A beheaded pez dispenser. Lip gloss. Buttons. Receipts. A pink bow. Three plastic forks. And a partridge in a pear tree.

"Ooooooooh," came the sound from near my left elbow. It was my daughter.

Oh, no. Look away. Just look away, honey.

"My pig!" she yells, pointing to a twisted pink pipe cleaner with one jiggly plastic eye glued to it. "You killed it!"

I vaguely remember pulling a pink pipe cleaner pig with jiggly plastic eyes from the slobbery jaws of our Bassett and stashing it in the junk drawer seconds before my daughter came into the kitchen.

"Where's his other eye?" she asked, holding the mangled pink thing in her tiny hand and turning it around. I rummaged through the drawer. Surely that eye was in here somewhere. Nope. It was doggie food.

"Maybe this will work," I offer, holding up a blue button. She shakes her head no. A pom pom? No. A penny?

On second thought, I'd better save up my pennies. I skimmed the drawer for more money. Quarters. Nickels. Dimes. I scooped them up and put them in a plastic baggie.

"You're not going to throw that away?" My son had arrived at my right elbow. Panic struck his face as he peered into the drawer and pointed to an unidentifiable plastic half-broken gadget tossed aside from some happy meal. What was it?

"What is it?" I asked.

"It's a... thing," he said. "I need it. I use it all the time."

He uses it all the time, even though it's been buried in the bottom of the drawer for at least six months, tangled in kite string and a paper clip.

"Take it," I said, knowing full well I'd find it on the playroom floor later and throw it away.

So there we stood, me separating trash from treasure in the junk drawer while my two offspring gave me instructions in stereo.

"I need that." It was half of a Lego space man.

"I want that." It was a tweety bird note pad with no feet.

"I've been looking for that." It was the top off a baby food jar

Enough, already.

"Enough already!" I tell them and banish them from the kitchen. Sulking and clutching the things they just couldn't live without, they leave me to continue putting things in my little piles. To Keep. To Throw Away. To Think About.

An hour later.

All is said and done and the drawer is empty. My Keep Pile is larger than my Throw Away Pile. I toss it back into the drawer. My Think About Pile is pretty hefty, too. I toss it back in, as well.

My plastic baggie filled with coins is quite impressive. What will I do with it?

"Mommy," comes a voice from behind me. "Did you find his other eye?"

One jiggly eye, that's what I'll buy. Then, perhaps I'll buy myself a pen. After all, that's what got me here in the first place.

Send him off to camp

If my daddy were here, he'd say you could ride to town on my bottom lip.

In other words, I'm pouting.

I dropped my nine-year-old at camp this week. I unpacked his trunk, made his bunk, fluffed his pillow, hugged the breath out of him and reminded him fourteen times that his extra socks and sweatshirts were in his duffle under his bed before leaving him in the beautiful mountains of Alabama.

He's great. I, on the other hand, have seen better days.

"You should be happy knowing he's having so much fun," says my husband, seeing my long face.

"I am," I tell him.

"You know he'd just be bored hanging around here all summer," he tells me.

"I know."

"He's learning cool new things and making new friends. He'll come home knowing how to do more for himself," he says.

"You're right."

"He doesn't need you around all the time," he adds.

"Shut up."

"You baby him too much," he goes on.

"No, really... Shut up."

"You don't want him to be a mama's boy."

That's it. Why don't I just send you off for a few weeks this summer, I want to tell him.

Hmmmm. Summer camp for husbands. You pack them up, drop them off and they come home knowing how to do more for themselves. I like it, I really like it.

I'd pay good money if my other half could go to a camp where he learned how to wash and fold clothes, clean a bathroom and effectively find something by himself in the refrigerator.

Case in point.

"Where's the mustard?"

"It's in the refrigerator," I tell him. No, he says, it's not. He's standing there, refrigerator door open, glaring.

"Yes, it is," I tell him.

"We don't have any," he declares, shutting the door. I walk into the kitchen. Open the refrigerator. Move the milk carton two inches to the right and, it's a miracle! Mustard! He couldn't find it because it would have required him to actually move something else in order to see it.

The same goes for anything he's looking for in a drawer, a closet or a cabinet. If it's not right on the top or doesn't jump out at him when he opens the door, he's says it's not there.

At fantasy husband camp, he'd learn how to find his own blue socks – right after arts and crafts, where he discovers the joy of helping create a second grade family tree project complete with photos, border and a snazzy theme.

Never again will I hear, "That's a mom thing" when deadline approaches and we still have blank posterboard.

I pose the possibility to him one night after e-mailing our son.

"Wouldn't it be great if I could send you off to camp?" I ask.

His eyes light up remembering, I am sure, his days of youth when he spent summers in the mountains, himself.

I was wrong.

"Could we sit around and drink beer all day and watch football?" he asks.

"No," I tell him.

"Could we sleep late and everybody had their own television and remote?" he continues.

"No."

"Could there be a Hooters at the camp and all the counselors were Victoria's Secret super models? Can we play golf all morning and hunt and fish in the afternoon and walk in with our muddy boots on and have a steak waiting served up by a Sports Illustrated swimsuit model and....."

On second thought, maybe this camp thing isn't such a good idea. After all, he'd never be able to find his extra socks.

"Oh, my Victoria's Secret super model counselor would help me find them," he assures me.

That's it. No fantasy husband camp for him this summer.

I just hope I can get my deposit back.

Please Mr. Postman

I've come upon a new exercise regime. I call it the My Son Hasn't Written Me From Camp workout and it goes something like this.

You walk to the mailbox and place your lovingly penned card addressed to your one and only son gently inside of it. Lift up the little red flag. Open the box to check just once more that you've put a stamp on it. Close it.

Walk back inside the house. Pass by the front door six times to see if the little red flag's been placed down, meaning the mail has been delivered. Walk briskly back down to the mailbox and stand, feet shoulder width apart, in front of it. Open it.

Reach inside, grab the mail. Exhale. Quickly sort through the envelopes and magazines. Nothing. Sort again. Nothing. Open the mailbox to see if you've left any inside. Close it. Open it again. Look. Close it.

Walk back to the house. Throw the mail on the desk. Sigh.

I call it My Son Hasn't Written Me From Camp workout because I've done the same thing every day since he's been gone. Sigh. No letter, yet.

There is another, more advanced, step to the workout. I've added it just since Saturday. It's the Threaten To Maim Your Husband look you throw in at the end, right after he asks you if you got any mail, grins and holds up a tattered piece of notebook paper scribbled with a few precious sentences.

You see, my husband got a letter. Addressed to him. Only to him. Not Dear Mom and Dad. Not Dear Dad and Mom. Just Dear Dad.

I was happy for him. I really was.

Dear Dad, he wrote. I'm having fun, he said. Keep sending the Braves scores.

Aha!

His dad has been emailing him the baseball scores which, to my son, is golden. I, on the other hand, have been emailing him the play-by-play action of the dog.

Dear Son, I wrote. I hope you're having fun, I said. Buddy ate some of your sister's silly putty today. We wonder if he'll bounce.

Obviously, the information I've been sending to camp isn't interesting enough. Although my daughter and I did wonder if we sat the dog on the funny papers, would it leave a picture on his rear end?

But I must change my strategy. No more sending stories of the dog's antics. No more telling him the exciting goings on of how we had beans for supper and I bought him a new toothbrush. They tell you to make life seem boring at home so the campers won't get homesick. Sad thing is, those are about the most exciting things that have happened since he left. It's a really cool toothbrush.

But I know the secret now.

Dear Son, I wrote. The Braves are doing fine, I said. Looks like Javy may make the All-Star game.

Then I cut all the articles out of the newspapers, put them in an envelope, and sent them to him.

"Where's the sports page?" my husband asked last night.

"I sent it to camp," I said. He laughed at me. "You're bribing him," he said. Bribing? Hardly. But maybe I could convince Javier Lopez to actually visit him at camp and tell him to write home to his mother...

I'll just keep hanging in there. I'll get a letter. And not because I send him the box scores, but because he loves me.

But if another week goes by and I still don't get one... maybe I'll write and tell him that his dad ate silly putty. That might work.

After all, if he keeps teasing me with the letter our son wrote him, then silly putty will be his only choice for dinner.

I wonder if he'll bounce.

Cow poker

O il changed. Car cleaned. Bag packed and loaded. We're all set for a mini trip to north Alabama to pick up our camper.

"The remote!" yells my six-year-old, eager to find the little gray-buttoned gadget that will help get her through five and a half hours of her mother's driving. "I can't find it!"

Whew! It's under the seat. I fumble through the box of tapes stashed in the back. Scooby Doo. Stuart Little.

"Let's start out with Parent Trap," I suggest, praying with both sets of fingers and a few toes crossed that she doesn't want to watch that sing-a-long tape that drives me crazy and ends up being stuck in my head for days. Oh, that's right. I hid that one someplace she'd never find it.

"This one," she says, handing me – what else? – the sing-a-long tape. "I found it in your closet."

I need a new hiding place.

I guess I should be grateful that my children have something to hold their interest in the car on long trips. Seems all the new family vehicles have DVD players built right in. Our version of the family road trip entertainment center is a tiny television-VCR combo we plug into the cigarette lighter and tie down with bungee cords. Not glamorous, but it works.

Ahhh, but I do miss the good old days of my youth where vacations in the family station wagon often led to blood being drawn over someone's elbow crossing the imaginary "my personal space" line. There were six of us, after all.

We didn't have televisions in our car in those days. Geez, I remember not even having to wear seat belts. I recall vividly, more than once, hurdling over the front seat trying to get away from a rabid sister whom I'd just "breathed on" all the while my mother drove down the highway.

Thank God for the seat belt law.

But what did we do for entertainment? Many things, as I recall.

There was Tortue Your Sibling. My husband has fond memories of his sister and him telling their little brother that the people in the car behind them were his real parents trying to catch up with them. That's just mean.

There's something about being held in a car for hours on end with only pork rinds and Pepsi for sustenance that brings out the worst in children.

We read comic books. We tried to sleep. But you only have to get a Cheeto stuck up your nose one time to realize that's not a good idea.

Perhaps my favorite thing to do on long trips, though, could be summed up in two words. Cow Poker.

You know the game – where you take one side of the road and someone else has the other and whenever you pass a cow pasture you count as many cows as you can and the one who has the most at the end of the trip wins.

Only, there are consequences. Like if you pass by a graveyard, you lose all your cows. But if you have a lone chimney on your side of the road, you get 200 more, or something like that. Everyone has their own version, I suppose.

Thankfully, my kids will turn off the television to play a rousing game of cow poker now and then. It forces them to look at the world around them, see the beautiful countryside, witness God's glory... and, if they get bored and start to breathe on each other, all I have to do is pull over.

I'm sure their real parents in the car behind us will be glad to take them for a while.

Who woodth idth be?

I have a confession to make. I'm not too proud of it, but it's true.

I watch the Bachelor.

You know... that show where the fella is swarmed by dozens of women who are all vying for the chance to become his wife. I can't explain why I'm drawn to it. I just am.

I've often wondered if my own husband would have chosen me if we'd met under those same circumstances. So, I asked.

"What if you were surrounded by all those women who wanted to marry you and you could have your pick... would you still pick me?"

At first, he tried to act like he didn't understand me. Bring on the visuals.

"All those women are wanting to marry you..." I point to the television where a dozen women in bikinis are bouncing around a hot tub drinking champagne.

"And then there's me." I point to myself wearing old sweat pants, a t-shirt and my retainer, sitting on the sofa drinking iced tea out of a Winnie the Pooh cup.

"You can have your pick. Who would it be?"

Only, I'm wearing my retainer, so it sounds something like... "Who woodth idth be?"

He looks at the television. Then he looks at me. He looks at the television. Then he looks at... the television.

Bikinis and champagne? Sweat pants and retainer?

"I'd have to have more information," he says finally. He's stalling. "Do they like sports?"

It all comes down to sports.

When we first got married, I was good at pretending that I knew something about football and basketball. I'd read the newspaper or watch just enough ESPN to throw out a name or two to impress him.

By the time he realized I knew nothing about sports it was too late. He was stuck with me. He's often said he should have given me a quiz before we got married to see just how much I knew.

How many people are on a football team? Who played in last year's Final Four? What's a wide receiver? A full court press?

Uhhhhh...

It can go both ways, you know, I tell him. There are a few things I would have liked to have known, as well.

Do you know how to replace an empty toilet paper roll with a full one? Do you iron your own clothes? Will you eat spaghetti twice a week for the rest of your life without complaining? Will you put the milk jug back in the refrigerator even though it's empty?

All things that would have been helpful to know, I think. Especially the toilet paper one.

I wonder if the girls on the Bachelor have thought to ask those questions. They would if they're smart. Then again, if they're smart they wouldn't be on the Bachelor.

But I watch it, all the same.

"So honey, have you decided whether or not you'd pick me over all those girls?" I ask. For argument's sake, I've told him that all the girls on the television show can name everyone in last year's Final Four, know every position on a football team and have season tickets to every major football game in the country, including the Super Bowl.

"And they can cook and keep a wonderful house and do all of this wearing high heels and without sweating," I add.

"So, it's any one of them...," I say, pointing to the television where they're now eating strawberries and sunbathing. "And then there's me."

It's not fair, I know. But sometimes you just have to ask.

He smiles. And, of course, he gives the right answer. He may not be able to operate an iron, but he's no fool.

Who would it be?

Retainer and all, idth woodth be me.

No butts about it

"Who are you and what have you done with my son?"

I'm walking through the den the other afternoon, collecting stray shoes and paper footballs from underneath the Christmas tree when I'm stopped dead in my tracks by 9 little words.

"Mom, can I help you clean up or anything?"

Did that just come out of the mouth of my nine-year-old son? I have to sit down.

"I have to sit down," I say. "Who are you and what have you done with my son?" I ask and peek under the sofa. He laughs.

"Mom," he says, drawing it out into two syllables like he does when he's aggravated with me.

Of course, I tell him. "You can clean up your room and help me fold clothes and pick up the yard...."

A ghastly look crosses his face – a cross between fear and amazement.

"Really?" he asks. I can tell he's disappointed. I wasn't supposed to actually take him up on his offer.

'Tis the season for being good, after all.

Our children are great all through the year, but put up a Christmas tree and start putting presents underneath and they become super charged, offering to help before being asked, taking extra good baths and eating green beans without gagging.

They even offer compliments... of sorts.

"Mommy, you could win that contest."

We are driving through town and late Sunday afternoon shopping traffic. Just the two of us – my daughter and I – leaving the grocery store on our way home. The radio is on.

"What contest?" I ask. I haven't been paying much attention to anything but the traffic light that won't seem to turn and the person dressed as a cow dancing in front of the steak house up ahead.

"The one on the radio," she says from the back seat. I look at her and she smiles that angelic little smile.

I turn up the radio in time to hear it, an advertisement for a Big Buck contest. Whoever bags the biggest deer wins.

"But I don't hunt, baby," I tell her and she wrinkles her brow like she doesn't understand.

"But your butt's big enough, mommy," she says. "Really, you could win."

I look in the rear view mirror. She's not laughing, just smiling that sweet little smile. She's six. And she meant it as a compliment... I think.

"Thank you, sweetie," I said. "But that's a contest for a big buck, not a big butt," I explain.

She thinks about it.

"Like a dollar?" she asks.

"No, like a deer," I say. "A big daddy deer with big antlers."

She appears disappointed that her compliment was futile, but suddenly recovers.

"Well, maybe they'll have a big butt contest and you can win," she says and points out the window. "There's that dancing cow man!"

I'm torn. Should I take this opportunity to explain to her that it's not nice to tell people you think they have a big caboose? Or should I take my left handed compliment and leave it at that?

I decide on the latter.

"Thank you, baby," I tell her. "You're such a sweet girl."

She smiles again. "Do you think Santa thinks so?" she asks.

"Santa thinks so," I assure her and she's visibly pleased.

Even Santa appreciates a compliment now and then.

I Want That

There are a couple of new kids in town. Their names are I Want That and I'm Gonna Get That. They showed up at my house about a month ago and I haven't been able to get rid of them since.

I overheard a conversation between the two just last night. I wish I could say that they were deeply enthralled in an educational documentary delving into the mysteries of the animal kingdom, but I can't lie. They were watching Scooby Doo.

"I want that," said I Want That, 5, as Barbie sashays across the television screen and chats with pals in coordinating mini skirts while having her hair done up in sparkly star barrettes that you, too, can put in your own hair.

I love the disclaimers that flash across the bottom of the screen during most toy commercials. They don't always tell the whole story.

Disclaimer: Dolls do not walk or talk on their own. Ken (why is he at the beauty salon, anyway?) doll and some accessories not included. You're gonna have trouble getting their shoes on.

"You don't need that," said I'm Gonna Get That, who is eight.

"But I want that," said I Want That.

"You want everythi..... Oooh, I'm gonna get that," said I'm Gonna Get That as Barbie leaves the screen and two cool kids sprawled on some floor shoot tiny cars through a twisting and turning race track featuring faux flames and simulated racing sounds in the most action packed afternoon of their lives.

Disclaimer: Cars may be smaller than they appear. Faux flames and action packed afternoon not included. Some assembly required. (Go ahead, admit it. You have to put the whole dang blasted thing together and at least one part's not gonna fit right.)

"You already have that," said I Want That.

"It's not like THAT," said I'm Gonna Get That. "I'm gonna get THAT."

And so it goes, for the next three and a half minutes before their educational documentary returns and Scooby comes back in full shudder over a ghost that is actually Farmer Doug with a flashlight. He was going to take back the farm before those nosy kids and their big goofy dog came along, you know.

I Want That and I'm Gonna Get That are quiet until the next commercial break begins.

I know, I know. They shouldn't be watching television, anyway. I agree. They watch far too much of it. That's what advertisers are hoping for – moms like me that let their kids watch cartoons.

I recall days of my youth when I morphed into I Want That at the mere mention of an Easy Bake Oven.

Disclaimer: The light bulb is hot. It tells you so on the box. Don't be like me and have to touch it to make sure. It's common sense. It's hot. Trust me.

If you want to know the truth, I think it's a fun part of Christmas to see all the toy and cool gadget commercials and think you want everything.

It's cute for kids. It doesn't work for everyone

"I want that," my husband says as yet another Victoria's Secret commercial slinks its way between episodes of his weekly educational documentary delving into the complexities of man – a.k.a. Saturday afternoon football.

Disclaimer: Victoria's Secret ensemble may be smaller than it appears. Your wife's body will not suddenly and miraculously look like the model's just because she puts the garment on

"You already have that," I remind him jokingly.

"It's not like THAT," he says, pointing to the TV.

That's it.

It's Scooby Doo for him from now on.

Close your eyes

My son sat down at the kitchen table to do his homework the other night. In minutes, he was in the den next to me and the fire, cross legged in the yellow chair clutching his blue notebook.

"Mom, what do you think about peppermint?" he asked me.

"I like peppermint," I said.

That wasn't good enough.

"No," he said. "Tell me what you think of it, really."

Seems his English teacher had given the fourth graders a writing assignment and from one 10 letter word they were supposed to come up with a few descriptive paragraphs.

"You can do it," I told him. "Just close your eyes. Sometimes you see things better that way."

Like Christmas trees when you were little.

Piling in the truck. Butterflies in your stomach. Finding the perfect tree is most important, after all. Riding to the farm, past scrub bush covered pastures and pine trees up to there. Past bare plum bushes and red clay ditches. We all pile out.

Someone remembers the perfect cedar perched alongside the fence round about here. We tromp through the woods. Thank goodness for extra socks. Pine straw crunches underneath our feet. It smells like Christmas.

Icy air mixed with upturned moss and fresh cedar. A holly berry tree tucked between the pines. A cedar, not quite perfect, but just the right size, calling out to us.

Thin metal teeth cutting through the tree trunk. Back and forth, back and forth. A cuss or two. It cracks. The tree's down.

Look up. We plug our ears with our fingers as the sound of the shotgun echoes through the woods and shards of mistletoe rain down upon us.

Trek back to the truck, through crunchy brown leaves and low lying briar bushes. See your breath. Thank goodness for extra socks.

Pile in the back, plucking beggar lice and burrs from your jeans. Clutch the tree, sticky and soft, so it doesn't fall out. Pockets full of mistletoe. It's time to go home.

I can remember it much better if I close my eyes. I can't see it, but I can hear it, smell it....

Like peppermint. Not just Christmas, but every Sunday of another time.

High, rainbow colored windows and velvet cushions. The choir sings. The preacher rises to begin his sermon. Like clockwork, without fail, somewhere from the morning crowd it comes. Painfully loud.

The crackle. The crinkle. The slide of clear cellophane wrap between grown up fingers. It's not a child. There is no shhhhhh.

You couldn't see it, but you wondered. Was it melt-in-your-mouth soft peppermint, dissolving on their tongue all buttery sweet. Or was it a hard little candy disk with red and white spirals that lasted a bit longer if they were careful not to bite, making their nostrils all icy cool. Sweet and sticky. Slick and sharp against their tongue after the red's all gone and it's snowy white.

You held your breath until the crackle subsided, thinking how cool it would be if the preacher one day just stopped his sermon to ask if they'd brought enough to share with everyone.

"Maybe it's butterscotch," my sister once pondered.

It was peppermint. I knew it. It had to be.

"Don't look at things just with your eyes," I told my son. "See them with your whole heart."

63

Just close your eyes.

Finding Christmas

I'm finding Christmas.

I guess I never lost it completely, really, just little bits that slipped quietly away with the smiles of my grandparents and my father years ago. But I'm finding it again. In so many ways.

Not in shopping malls or movie theatres. Not in presents or commercials. It's not what credit cards can buy or I can order from my computer. It's not even the silly holiday songs that still make me laugh.

It's the little things.

Driving through the county on a recent cold December morning, I found Christmas.

It was a gray haired old gentleman in a tattered brown coat who walked down the railroad tracks with a cane wrapped in silver tinsel.

It was a once white trailer with rusted windows and a patched door lined in brilliantly colored Christmas lights.

It was the backyard clothesline filled with work pants and dingy white tees and underwear, too, with one pair of bright red and green striped socks flapping in the wind. It was the wreath on the tractor with mud-caked tires parked in the field beside the roadside.

I'm seeing Christmas everywhere I go.

It's the lady at the gas station in her jingle bell necklace humming Joy To The World as she fills up her car. It's the little girl's mouth all sticky with peppermint kissing the car window. It's the little boy waddling into school wearing three layers of clothes, a scarf and a pom pom hat that covers his eyes. It's the cashier at the grocery store smiling and laughing as her Christmas bulb earrings light up her face.

It's the sound of the bell ringers as you run to the grocery store. It's the clink of the coins as they're dropped in the bucket.

It's the glow of the fire barrel at the Christmas tree lot and the heady smell of pine filling your head as you walk through the rows. It's seeing trees tied to car tops with twine. It's pulling boxes out of the attic and uncovering treasures forgotten since last year, tangled in lights, bent hooks and year old candy canes.

It's finding photos of your babies in frames of construction paper and reindeer stickers. It's remembering where you got what and how long you've had that. It's an expensive handpainted ball sharing a limb with a notebook paper heart covered in glitter.

It's not moving a single ornament placed by tiny hands, even if two thirds of them are on the bottom.

It's unwrapping the manger scene and placing baby Jesus in just the right spot where he doesn't get cold and the cat doesn't lick him. It's making sure Mary is close so if he cries she can pat him and tell him it's all right. It's discussing what the three wise men have in those boxes and deciding it might have been nice if they'd bought him some candy.

It's putting a Santa hat on the dog. It's a pig that snorts We Wish You A Merry Christmas sitting next to the sofa.

It's tucking your children in tight and having them ask if you really think Santa saw everything they did today. It's kissing their forehead and telling them not to worry, Santa gives them a break every now and then.

It's when the house is all quiet. You turn out the lights and stare at the tree, at paper made angels with handprints for wings.

That's when you'll find Christmas. Not in shopping malls or movie theatres. Not presents or commercials. Not with your credit card or on your computer.

You'll find it in the little things. All you have to do is look.

I've got the fever

I've got the fever. The baby fever.

I can't say that too loudly, though, because the last time I announced I had the fever my husband bought me a dog. Take two aspirins and buy a Bassett Hound was his remedy.

"It's just like having a baby," he said. He was talking about Buddy, our big, goofy four-legged family member that barks at grass and howls at squirrels. He arrived at our house around Christmas, not long after I muttered the words, "Wouldn't it be nice to have another baby?"

As a pup, Buddy waddled around the house on his little dumpy legs. His ears were always dripping wet because they got in his water bowl whenever he tried to take a drink. I admit, he was cute.

"See, isn't that just like having another baby?" my husband asked. He was proud of himself. I thought of reminding him that our two human children never barked at grass at 2 a.m. or had stealth gas that could clear out a room in five seconds flat, but I didn't.

Instead I shot him The Look and dropped the subject of having more children for a while.

I come by wanting a big family honestly, I suppose. There are six of us. Girl. Girl. Boy. Girl. Girl. Boy.

I'm that fourth girl. I was supposed to be a boy, though. Legend has it that on the day I was born, my father called home to tell the other siblings of my joyous arrival. My brother picked up a kitchen chair and threw it across the room shouting, "I told that woman not to have another girl!"

I've often wondered if that is just one of those childhood legends that gets passed down through the years and grows more dramatic with each new audience. It surfaces at family gatherings and, admittedly, I've told it to my own children.

"Didn't your brother like you?" my daughter asks.

"I know how he felt," my son stoically proclaims, looking at his sister.

My brother liked me, I explain. It's just that he already had three sisters and was ready for a little brother, which he got later.

I don't even know if my older brother recalls throwing the chair across the kitchen, but the tale is indelibly burned into our collection of family stories and will thus be passed along for generations.

"What did he do when I was born?" my daughter asks of her own brother, who was three years old at the time.

"He loved you very much," I tell her as he rolls his eyes. Honestly, he did, but it was the purple-trimmed tennis shoes that his grandmother bought him later that day that he loved more at the moment.

"I don't remember those shoes," he tells me. One – he really doesn't remember or Two – he selectively refuses to admit that he once liked Barney The Dinosaur, thus the purple tennis shoes.

"What did he say about me?" my daughter asks.

"He said you were beautiful," I tell her. Actually, for weeks after she was born we would pass by the hospital on our way into town and he would say, "OK, it's time to take her back now."

I had to explain that his new sister wasn't like a library book.

Did I mention that I have the fever? It's creeping up on me, I suppose, because I'm getting older. I'm hoping that our newest niece or nephew, scheduled to arrive any day now, will help sate my desire to have just one more of my own.

And if not... I guess there's always Buddy.

"See, isn't it just like having another baby?"

I recall those words now as Buddy slobbers on my foot. Maybe it's best I just keep my fevers to myself for a while. There's no telling what I'd do if another puppy showed up at our house.

I just might end up with one less kitchen chair.

You to remind me

I used to think there was nothing better than walking barefoot, jumping over the cracks in the sidewalk downtown on a summer afternoon when the pavement was hot and the mosquito bites on your ankles itched so badly you had to stop every few steps to scratch.

The doors on Main Street stood wide open and you could hear the big fans whirr at the back of the stores as you walked by. On Saturday night, paper funeral home fans cut through the evening heat as the auctioneer spilled over the chairs and books and tables in the antique store.

You could cut your bike through the crooked little dirt road almost any day it hadn't rained and be clear across town before you'd sucked the red off a fireball. And a dug up weed with tiny yellow flowers fit nicely in a cracked coffee cup from way back in the cabinet and looked beautiful in its spot on the kitchen table.

Honeysuckle crept wildly and furiously along the rusty barbed wire, and a tiny clever hand lent tastes and smells of sweetness as pure as the afternoon rain that pelted you as you ran home from a swim, wet hair clinging to your neck and sunburned, freckled shoulders.

The soft voices from the television would waft under your doorway, left open in the night so the light would dribble in and chase monsters away. Your last thoughts before sleep placed its soft hand across your eyes were of when you'd be old enough to sit up until the late news came on, and you wondered if the hard, plastic eyes of your tattered bear really blinked in the darkness like your brother said they did.

The twisted look on your neighbor's face when he tasted the bright yellow lemonade you poured into the tiny Dixie cup made you laugh. And the dollar he gave you got washed in your shorts and came out all faded, but sat in your bank hidden under your bed for a week.

The sky looked so big and the clouds seemed so soft. And the moon was so close, and the stars and the rainbows. You were sure if you could only stand on top of the house or even the swingset you could touch them and hold them and keep them forever.

The pink washcloth was cool against your forehead and the soft smell of Oil of Olay washed over your hurt as your mother stroked back your hair and tucked the covers up close around you. Her warm palm against your cheek made you feel all better.

And daddy's laugh when you asked him if Hank Aaron was good made you feel like the world was all safe and nice, and the strength of his arms when he hugged you good-bye and the smell of the leather of his boots made you know it was true.

If I dig deep enough, I remember those things.

"I found this just for you," she said just the other day, her tiny fingers covered in dirt. Clutched in her fist was the most beautiful green weed with tiny yellow flowers. It fit nicely in the old coffee cup from way back in the cabinet, and when we placed it on the kitchen table she sat and looked at it in awe.

"It's really pretty, isn't it mommy?" she asked. And I said yes. And I told her of how I used to pick the same pretty flowers and give them to my mother. That made her smile.

"I forget one time you were a little girl," she said and smiled again.

"Me, too," I said.

"I'm so glad I have you to remind me."

One of those days

I t was one of those days.

Dreary is the only way to describe it. Not raining, but drizzly. Not cold, but just cool enough to make you shiver.

I needed a pick me up and I was hungry. I knew just where to go.

"Did you know if you burp with your mouth closed then your head might blow off?"

"My brother can burp the alphabet."

"My dad burps."

"My mom burps."

"Moms don't burp. My mom said so."

"Well, my mom does. Really loud."

"My dog burps."

Really? I don't know that I'd ever heard a dog burp. I would have liked to find out a little more about the burping dog, but I thought it wise to try and change the subject.

"Is everyone enjoying their chicken?" I interject. I am having lunch with my daughter and her kindergarten pals.

"I don't eat chicken."

"Why did the chicken cross the road?"

"I can't cross the road without holding a grown up's hand."

"My cousin's hand has warts on it. They're gross. They're all slimy sometimes."

Time to change the subject again. We are eating, after all.

"Have you been outside to play today?" I ask no one in particular.

"No, it was too wet."

"I jumped in a mud puddle yesterday and got in trouble. My shoes were all wet."

"I got new shoes. See?"

"Don't put your foot on the table. It's not nice."

"Yes," I agreed. "It's not nice to put your foot on the table. But those are cool shoes."

"My brother got new shoes and I think they cost a bagillion dollars."

Wow.

"Wow," I said. "That is a lot."

"Hey," said a little voice beside me. "What does is mean?"

Hmmmm.

"Is means.... Is means.... Is," I explain rather well, I think. "You know, is is something that just is. Understand?"

"No."

"No."

"Nope."

They are ganging up on me.

"Hey, did you know his dog burps?" I asked, pointing to the little fella across the table. Diversion. It worked.

"My dog eats cat food."

"My mama is still mad at my dog for doing something he wasn't supposed to do."

"What'd he do?" I had to ask.

He whispered in my ear. Gross.

"Gross," I said. It was time to go.

"Let's pick up our milk cartons and put them on our tray," I said.

"I can make milk come out of my nose. Wanna see?"

I shake my head no as we push our chairs back under the table.

"I sneezed one time and milk came out of my nose."

"I sneezed so hard one time a pea came out of my nose."

"I don't eat peas."

It was one of those days. Not raining, but drizzly. Not cold, but cool enough to make you shiver.

I had needed a pick me up and I found it. I found out a lot, actually.

Did you know if you burp with your mouth closed your head might blow off?

You do now.

A natural wonder

My husband's brother and his wife are expecting their first child early this summer. Everyone's excited, especially the other grandchildren. When my five-year-old exclaimed, "I can teach the baby everything!" I got to thinking.

Should I warn them?

I'm no expert, mind you. I still bow to the great mothers of the world who can cease a whine with a mere look – that half glance/half stare that makes misbehaving children stop cold. I've even seen husbands succumb to it.

"How'd you do that," I asked a friend when her husband suddenly changed his tune from 'I'm playing golf tomorrow' to 'I think I'll work in the yard tomorrow.'

"The Look," she revealed. "Master it and you can control the world."

I try. Lord, how I try.

"What's wrong with your face?" I get from my son when I try it on him. My five-year-old gives it back to me. It doesn't work on my husband. Yet.

There are the books you can buy to help with the regular child-rearing things, like diaper changing and feeding schedules.

Not once, however, did I read anywhere how to dislodge Batman from the toilet, or what to do when your child eats a Dentyne gum wrapper.

"Just keep checking," my mother said when I called her in a panic. "You'll see it again."

What a way to spend the day, nervously waiting for your one-year-old's next you- know-what. But, ew, she was right.

That was with my first child. By the time the second one came along, I had relaxed a little bit.

When my daughter toddled toward me one day with dog food clutched in one hand and Purina crumbs around her mouth, my first thought was, "Don't eat the dog food! We're almost out!"

I must admit, though, there are days now when I wish my children would eat something as nutritious as dog food. Eat anything, for that matter.

New mothers, beware: Children can go from wanting carrots or chicken nuggets or peanut butter for every meal to suddenly proclaiming, "I don't like that."

You learn to appreciate what little nutritional value you can find, too. Technically, ketchup is a vegetable, right? Some days it's so bad you convince yourself that an orange tic tac has to have some hidden vitamin. It's orange-flavored, isn't it? Hey, you take what you can get.

Never did I read in my child rearing books how to react when my child stuck cheese toast up his nose. Not once did I discover the intellectual way to explain that it's not nice to run around the house naked with underwear on your head. Will my husband ever learn?

Just kidding.

I did, however, learn very quickly that my body produces the most amazing substance that no man will ever possess.

Mother Spit.

It can take the Cheeto residue right off a mouth and make a cowlick cringe. It might even take tar off a car if you needed it to. I wouldn't be surprised.

It's a natural wonder, it is.

I think I'll wait until my sister-in-law asks for my advice before I offer any. Life's little surprises, especially when it comes to children, are what keep us all on our toes.

Until then, I'll just keep practicing my Look, seeking the nutritional value in chewing gum and trying to figure out how to get Play-Doh off the dog.

Hey, I wonder if a little spit would work? It's worth a try.

I wore a purple shirt

I wore a purple shirt.

It used to be one of my favorites, light purple with tiny white pinstripes and sleeves just the right length that I could roll up when it was still warm out. It wasn't cold that day or even chilly. And I kept pushing my sleeves up and pulling them down all day.

Nervous, I guess.

It was morning. I was at my son's school and we were having a meeting in the lunchroom about an upcoming event - a group of mothers planning a Christmas bazaar, talking about tickets and last night's homework assignments. I went to the office to call and ask a friend a question. She wouldn't make it to the meeting, she said. She couldn't get away from the television. And she told me what had happened.

One had hit.

The rest of a day is a blur, but I remember my son's principal coming into the lunchroom a few minutes later and telling us another one had hit. I remember sitting there, looking around the room at mothers just like myself and suddenly I thought how helpless we all were. Strong, adult women who could take care of children and homework and houses and husbands and work full time jobs and even find time to volunteer and help our neighbors. And suddenly, we were helpless.

My gut hurt. I can close my eyes now right this very second and I can't feel it but I can remember it. I don't remember ever having it hurt quite that way before.

I remember taking my son to football practice that afternoon and sitting on a blanket in the grass as my daughter drew on notebook paper beside me. When the sound of an airplane sneaked through the clouds I remember locking eyes with another mother nearby, a stranger, and knowing that at that exact moment we were feeling the same thing.

We all slept in the same bed that night. Our two children snuggled up between us. I didn't close my eyes.

Because when I did, I thought about the parents who just the week before, the day before, may have taken their sons to football practice. And the mothers who were planning on helping out with their children's holiday bazaar. But now they couldn't.

Would my children remember this day? Probably.

My sister and her friend were playing with Barbies on the living room floor and I was sitting beside them watching television the day Richard Nixon left office. I remember that.

We were building onto our house and I was carrying my baby brother around the yard because he wanted to watch the workmen lay brick. There was red clay everywhere and my feet were all muddy. The workmen had a radio on and they interrupted music to tell everyone that Elvis had died. I remember one of the men started to cry.

And I remember sitting at my high school lunch table with my friends, talking and eating and just being 17. Our coach came into the lunchroom and announced the space shuttle had exploded. I had a science test that day.

It's funny what your mind chooses to remember.

This day was different, in so many ways. And it always will be.

I wore a purple shirt.

I don't wear it anymore.

Take your medicine

I hope nobody's looking.

Here I stand on this sunny morning, on the porch with both feet planted firmly on either side of my squirming basset hound, holding his mouth shut with both hands while his head bobs up and down, waiting for him to swallow a big, yellow pill.

Ew. Dog slobber. And it's running down my arm. I lift my right leg and attempt to swipe it off on the knee of my jeans.

"What are you looking at?" I ask our lab, who's decided he needs to find out what this crazy lady's doing over here on the porch.

The basset hound squirms. Surely he's swallowed it by now.

I release my grip on his jowls and he looks up at me. I'm proud of myself. I gave the dog his medicine.

"Ffpth."

Ffpth – that's the sound the dog makes when he spits the big, yellow pill onto the brick and then looks up at me with those sad basset hound eyes. He can't bark at me. He has tonsillitis.

He looks at me. He looks at the pill. The lab sniffs the pill. He looks at me. He looks at the pill.

I pick up the pill and the basset hound high tails it down the steps, where I tackle him in the front yard, open his mouth and put it back in.

"You are going to take this medicine," I proclaim out loud. I am sitting on the grass in the front yard in broad daylight with my legs wrapped in WWF fashion around a basset hound with tonsillitis while I hold his mouth shut with both hands and shout out demands as a lab sniffs around me.

"Stop sniffing me," I tell the lab. Ew, dog slobber.

I hope nobody's looking.

Three ffpths later, he swallows it. My job is done.

I should be used to it. My own children – the human ones – don't like taking medicine either.

When they were really little they used to push it out with their tongues while it dribbled down their chins. Then came the task of trying to figure out just how much medicine they actually swallowed and how much more I had to give them.

Those times were stressful.

Especially stressful if it was some of that expensive stuff – one of those super duper antibiotics that surely must be made of ground up diamonds and one hundred dollar bills because it cost so much.

When they spit out the Tylenol, that's one thing. When they spit out the expensive prescription stuff, that's when you're tempted to make them suck it off their shirt.

I've seen some of the most hideous faces come from taking bad tasting medicine. I've hidden medicine in applesauce. I've lied and said it tasted like bubble gum when it really tasted like soap. I've had to go to the bank and cash a check to pay my children to take their medicine.

All for the sake of their health.

My six-year-old still takes liquid medicine. Her older brother has graduated to pills.

Like the dog. Who has tonsillitis.

"Will you give the dog his medicine tonight?" I ask my husband after my morning wrestling match, during which I think I sprained something.

"You just weren't doing it right," he says and proceeds to take a pill, call the dog onto the porch, open his mouth, put his hand halfway down his throat, close his mouth and hold it there for a few seconds.

"See, you just weren't putting it in far enough," he boasts as I silently pray that the dog spits it back out. He doesn't.

"Good, then you can give him his medicine from now on," I proclaim.

"Admit it," he says. "You just weren't doing it right.'

"I just didn't...." I stammer.

"Admit it," he says.

"Okay, OK. I wasn't doing it right," I admit. Boy, that hurt.

What a day. First, the dog. Now I have to admit to my husband that he was right.

I hope nobody's looking.

Warming our souls

I wish it came in a box, so I could pull it out whenever I felt like it.

It's the smell... or maybe it's the sound... probably both, I suppose, combined with all of the other little things that thread together to form a blanket of memories for my soul.

Thanksgiving Day. As a child, it was magical. And if I search deep enough I can still hear it, feel it, taste it.

The hours before sunlight. Snuggled deep in layers of covers long before we ventured to put our own feet on the floor we would hear my mother padding around the kitchen.

The swish of her house coat . The oven door creaking open for a peek of the main attraction. The shuffle of pans for the bread and pots for the peas and the rice and the gravy that would soon be simmering softly on the back burners.

Smells. None are quite so perfect as those that waft from the kitchen and sneak under the doorways on Thanksgiving Day. The bird carefully checked each hour on the hour throughout the darkness of night is now the color of warm caramel. A heavenly cloud of warm, sweet goodness escapes with each opening of the oven.

Cornbread. Homemade cornbread, baked the night before and crumbled amongst onions and celery and eggs and all those other secret ingredients only your own mother knows. Baked to the peak of perfection, waiting to be smothered with gravy that bubbles with bits of eggs and broth and tender chicken.

Each one gets their favorite. All six of us. Green beans. Carrots. Tiny round green peas. I'm not sure who calls tiny green peas their favorite, but they're always there. And we always eat them. They are comfort food, and the day would not be the same without them.

The sweet potatoes. The desserts.

Creamy orange perfection tousled with melted butter and brown sugar and warmed by a blanket of tiny marshmallows. Crunchy sugared pecans tossed throughout pies trimmed in the flakiest crusts. Cakes – layers upon layers of chocolate and coconut. Bananas swimming in pudding, whipped cream and wafers.

But far greater than the feast before our eyes was the sating of our hearts. All of us, together. Always an extra seat or two set at the table for someone otherwise alone. Peace among chaos. That was our house.

I can still hear it. Taste it. Feel it.

But what makes these thoughts of Thanksgiving all the more precious is that every year another memory is added. Pine cones and construction paper turkey feathers. Fall leaves. My own children create these masterpieces and settle them on their grandmother's table. My husband asks for seconds of his favorite sweet potato casserole. Another voice wonders aloud, "Who really likes the little round green peas?" And then they eat them anyway.

Then the next day comes and another Thanksgiving is only a memory.

But every now and then my own children and I will snuggle up close and unfold that blanket of memories made larger each passing year.

And together we will warm our souls.

For this, I am most thankful

"Why do we close our eyes when we pray?" she asks me. We are sitting on the side porch steps, looking in the late afternoon sun for nothing in particular to happen.

"So we can be closer to God," I tell her.

She wrinkles her nose. There's a tiny new freckle right there beside it, I notice.

"You look like someone sprinkled brown sugar right here," I tell her and tickle across the bridge of her nose. She wrinkles it again and smiles. She climbs in my lap.

"I know what thankful means," she tells me.

"Tell me," I say and I begin to braid her hair, separating the thick brown strands in my fingers. Our neighbor's black cat peeks from the corner of their house.

"It means you're glad you have something and you want to say thank you," she says.

I tell her she's exactly right.

"Do you think dogs are thankful?" she asks me. There's an itch on her ankle and I help her scratch.

I think they are, I tell her. We decide that they're thankful for their yard and their food.

"And they're very happy when you play with them," I say.

She's quiet. Somewhere down the street a basketball is bouncing.

"What are you thankful for this Thanksgiving?" I ask her. She turns to look at me.

"Mommy," she says, "You shouldn't be thankful just one time a year. You should be thankful all the time."

I am impressed.

"Who taught you that?" I ask her. She gives a little laugh like I have lost my mind.

"I just know," she says. I squeeze her close.

"I'm thankful every day for you," I tell her.

She smiles. "I'm thankful every day for you," she says and we agree that we're glad we've all got each other, even when her brother picks on her and the boys make us watch football.

The dogs bark. That reminds her.

"I don't think he's thankful all the time when he has to clean out the poopie dog pen," she says of her brother.

"But think how thankful the dogs are that he does," I say and she shakes her head.

She's quiet again. I reach into my pocket for a rubber band to fasten her braid and wrap it around the end.

"Do dogs pray?" she finally asks me. She's been thinking about this, I can tell. My answer has to be good.

"I don't know if animals pray, but I know God takes care of them just the same," I tell her.

"And we can pray for them," I add. "We can always pray for them, just in case."

She closes her eyes.

"What are you doing?" I ask.

"Praying that the dogs get a big bone for Thanksgiving," she says. "I think that's what they'd pray for."

She opens her eyes just as the neighbor's cat dashes across the yard. She closes them again.

"I'm praying for that cat, too, so the dogs won't get him," she says. She makes me smile.

She opens her eyes and runs her fingers across my nose.

"It looks like someone sprinkled brown sugar right here," she says and a little girl giggle pops out. A little girl giggle pops out of me too, surprising even myself.

That's when it happens, when you're sitting on the side porch steps. Looking for nothing in particular, but finding everything you need.

For that, I'm thankful every day.

A guide to be good

My birthday was last week. As if turning 4 years shy of 40 wasn't enough, I was forced to entertain the thought that I may not be a good wife.

I arrived at this shortly after being asked where I'd like to go for my birthday dinner. I ask for only two things on my birthday – that I neither have to cook nor clean up after someone who has cooked for me. It's an innocent enough wish, I think, especially for someone who's practically middle-aged.

We were still thinking through our choices when my husband said, "Of course, if you were a good wife…" and glanced over to the white refrigerator door where an 8 by 10 sheet of paper hung - The Good Wife's Guide.

Apparently, or so it says, this guide appeared in Housekeeping Monthly in May of 1955. Some say it's a fake, another one of those made up internet stories that's been forwarded and re-forwarded through the years. Totally genuine or entirely bogus, it is still my husband's ultimate fantasy.

What he meant on this particular evening was that if I was a Good Wife, I would not be concerned about going out to dinner, even if it was my birthday. According to the guide, a Good Wife's number one concern is her husband. "Plan ahead, even the night before, to have a delicious meal ready on time for his return," it reads.

I do plan ahead. I plan the night before to eat the next day. And 5 times out of 7 I have a meal on the table. If only they hadn't included the word delicious, I'd be alright on this one.

Among several tips, the guide tells wives to, when he gets home from work, "take off his shoes... speak in a low, soothing and pleasant voice." It's hard to speak soothingly when you're holding your nose.

"Be a little more interesting for him," it says. Unless my name is A Rod and I've just scored a three point basket in the Super Bowl, that isn't going to happen.

"Make one last trip through the house just before your husband arrives. Run a dust cloth over the tables," it recommends. What's a dust cloth?

I've got this one wrapped up. "Minimize all noise. At the time of his arrival, eliminate all noise of the washer, dryer or vacuum." That noise can't be heard even when he's not home.

And my personal favorite: "Listen to him. Let him talk first – remember, his topics of conversation are more important than yours."

I'll try to remember this the next time he's rambling on about how turkey season's coming up and his lips are pursed together demonstrating chirping sounds while he's got a camouflage do-rag on his head.

Despite his attempts to make me a Good Wife, we went out to dinner on my birthday. Afterwards, I stood in front of the mirror counting my wrinkles and contemplating my new age. Is it me, or is my head getting bigger?

"Do you think my head is bigger?" I ask from the bathroom. No answer. I poke my head out the door. He's laying on the bed watching basketball. He looks at me.

"Did you say something, Bobblehead?" he asks.

He lived that night.

That, my friends, is a Good Wife.

It wouldn't be the same

I found my New Year's resolution early this year. It came to me one pre-Christmas afternoon.

"Stay close to me at all times," I directed my little crew as we made our way through the parking lot. A car stopped before the crosswalk and motioned us across. I waved back in thanks and hurried us along into the store, past holiday shoppers waiting on the other side to cross and through the whoosh of the electric door.

"Ride or walk?" I asked my six-year-old then picked her up anyway and deposited her in the back of the buggy. "Ride today," I said, surveying the thickening crowd. She scowled.

"I want to walk," she said, a pout emerging. I was quick on my feet today.

"Pretend you're the queen and I'm your driver," I suggested. She liked that idea and I silently apologized to her future husband.

"You two don't leave my sight," I told my son and his friend. They're nine.

"We're 9-years-old," my son informed me, like I'd forgotten.

"And your point would be?" I asked.

"We want to go look at the sports stuff," he said. "You're buying... groceries," he added, making a face like groceries was a bad word.

"No, I'd never forgive myself if I lost you one week before Christmas," I told them. "And I'm pretty sure your mom would never let you come over again," I said to his friend. "You both stay with me."

They growled.

"How many things do you have to get?" my son asked. I counted in my head. Milk. Coffee filters. Soap.

"Three," I tell them.

"Can we buy something?" he asks. "I've got my own money."

Good. Then he can help pay for the groceries, and I told him so.

"No way," he said. "It's only for things I need for myself. It's my own money."

His own money, hard earned by taking out the garbage, feeding the animals and cleaning out the dog pen. Hidden for weeks in some mysterious spot in his bedroom, only to be pulled out in secrecy and counted every now and then.

We meandered through the grocery aisles, my crew of three carefully surveying every purchase and berating me for every item over the initial three I'd quoted.

I agreed to one quick look through the sporting goods before we checked out.

"Do you see anything you want to buy?" I asked. "With your money, of course." He looked around. There was plenty he wanted, and most everything he could afford.

"No," he said. "I'll wait for something I really want."

We checked out without much ado, save for the back log at the front door waiting again in the cold air to cross the drive to the parked cars.

"Wait, mom," said my son as he put his arm in front of me to stop me from walking. I watched as from his pocket he pulled not pennies and dimes, but dollar bills, carefully folding them as he walked over to the red Salvation Army bucket and slid them into the tiny slot.

"I would have given you money for that," I told him as he came back over.

"It wouldn't be the same," he said. "It had to be mine."

Suddenly he looked older.

"I've made my New Year's resolution," I told my son later that night as I tucked him into bed. "I want to be more like you."

"Aw, mom," he said. "What'd you want to do that for?"

"Just because," I said and kissed him on the forehead.

Just because. Because it had to be his.

An exercise in translation

I won't swear to it, but I think the goldfish were laughing at me this morning as I stumbled half-asleep into the kitchen, one tennis shoe untied and the other tied too tightly. I sat down and rearranged my laces. Maybe they're just hungry, I decided, and tossed a few fish food flakes into their bowl in the center of the breakfast table. The two newest additions to the family sauntered to the surface.

Oh, but to be a fish, I thought. Not a care in the world except when their next pinch of a meal would come. The occasional scare when the kids decide to play drums with their pencils on the side of the bowl. The excitement of a stray fly swimming in circles on top of the water.

Then it hit me. I don't want to be a fish. I don't really want to sit here in the dark of early day contemplating the life of little Nemo and little Jessie. (Those are the names of our fish, by the way.)

I'm stalling. I can't get into gear to go for my morning walk.

This is all new to me, this getting up at the crack of day to walk the some-odd two and a half miles through the neighborhood and back home again, timing my return only moments before the sound of alarm clocks waft down the stairs. My friend and I decided to try this bout of early morning exercise to see how we liked it.

My husband was thrilled.

I must preface here. I have never been one to exercise consistently. Something else always got in the way.

Like children. And work. And there was that time I had to clean the lint trap in the dryer. I would come up with any and every excuse not to sweat.

"Exercise is good for you," he would say. That's what would come out of his mouth, but I would hear instead, "You need to get your fat rear end moving."

My husband hates my female-translator – that little device that sits in my subconscious and is triggered by the sound of his voice. It waits for him to say something seemingly harmless, then translates it into something destined to make me mad or pout or hide the remote control.

My translator's fueled primarily, I've decided, by lack of caffeine and lack of sleep, with a few hormones thrown in for good measure. It can turn itself on at any moment.

"Where did you get that skirt?" he asks.

"You don't like it. It's too tight. I'll change."

He usually stands there dumbfounded, afraid to speak. After twelve years, you'd think he'd learn. I've heard rumors that they never do.

So, he was quite happy when I decided to take up walking. He didn't even have to suggest it. And I've been happy with it, too. So on this day I leave the goldfish to their breakfast, grab my flashlight and push myself out the door.

Waiting at the corner for my walking buddy to arrive, I realize just how peaceful it is. Quiet, save for the dull sound of thunder miles away and a dog's bark a couple of streets over. There's something about seeing things before the light of day hits the pavement that makes you feel good.

Two-thirds of the way through our walk, the dull sound of thunder becomes more clear and rain begins to fall. Should we make a run for it? Nah. We just keep talking and walking, rain running down our backs.

An early bird on her way to work offers us two wet strangers a ride, but home's in sight. Thank you Mrs. Sculley.

I get home in time to dry off before the kids come dragging down the stairs.

"Aren't you glad you've started walking," offers my husband as he gets ready for a shower. Yes, I am, I admit out loud.

Is that really what he said? My translator kicks in.

"Are you saying I'm fat?" Only, the water's running and he can't hear me.

I think need some caffeine.

At the carwash

Here I go again, making a New Year's Resolution. I'm going to keep my car clean. How hard can it be?

Obviously, you've never spent the week with us, driving around the city to and fro. Collecting all sorts of interesting whatnots between and under the seats, hiding under the floor mats. A happy meal toy here, a pack of Skittles there. Newspapers. Legos. Barbie doll shoes.

In my heart of hearts, I believe gremlins hide under my car seats and in the darkness of night crumble cookies and create all this junk. I do believe I could subsist in my car for at least a couple of days if I ever had to. Like if I got stuck in the carwash..

"What if we get stuck in here?" my five-year-old asks, her eyes widening as soap suds dribble down the windshield and cover the car. I'd never really thought of that.

"We won't get stuck in here, honey," I say in my most consoling mother voice, the one I use when I'm trying to convince her watermelons aren't going to grow in her stomach just because she accidentally swallowed a seed. Her brother came up with that one.

She didn't seem convinced this time either.

"We won't get stuck in here," I go on. "But just in case... look, I've got half a pack of M&Ms right here between the seats. And look, there's a coloring book and four broken crayons in the floorboard in case we get bored. And here are two tissues and a flashlight. And look, a phone book with half the pages torn out..."

I was sure we could scrounge up a couple of fries under the back seat if we tried hard enough, too.

"But what would we drink?" she asks. The game was getting fun.

The big swirling brushes began their cleaning frenzy outside as we pondered our dinner options should we get stranded.

Sure enough, I turn around and there staring at me from the way back cup holder is a bottle of SunKist.

Perhaps I should explain "way back." I drive a Suburban. Now, I know there are those people who think SUV drivers are spawns of the devil. I actually heard someone on television recently try to argue that SUV drivers are un-American, selfish, egotistical maniacs.

Get a life. But I digress. Back to way back.

Way back is the third seat, where my son and his friends like to sit during carpool. It's far enough away from the front where they think I can't hear their conversations, but close enough where I really can. It's where my son leaves jackets and library books and tries to hide the good Sunday shoes he hates and sheds the second we get in the car.

It's where my two children can be far enough away from each other not to do bodily harm, but close enough where he can kick the back of her seat until she screams.

The car's being rinsed as my daughter and I decide that we could, indeed, live in the car if we got stuck. At least until the M&Ms ran out... or we had to go to the bathroom.

"There's no potty in here," she declares. "I gotta go. Now."

I've never been so happy to see the red light in the car wash turn to green.

I cleaned out my car over the weekend. All the Legos and Barbie shoes, French fries and goldfish crackers are gone.

Deep in the recesses of the way back I found an unopened pack of mints and stashed them in the console. Just in case. You never know when a trip to the car wash might go awry.

Backyard tendencies

O^{w!}

I wasn't expecting an audience.

"Mommy, what are you doing?!" shrieked my daughter as she entered the bathroom the other day. There I stood, hunched over the sink, my face an inch from the mirror, my head tilted back and one hand brazening a pair of tweezers dangerously close to my eyeball. I guess I looked kinda scary.

"I'm – Ow! – plucking my eyebrows," I tell her.

Ow! There goes another one. That one stung. I glance over and see her hovered in the corner, covering her own eyebrows and wincing like she's in pain.

"I thought you pluck chickens," she whispers, looking up at me, big eyes peeking from underneath her tiny hands.

"Yes, baby, you can pull the feathers off of chickens. But women also – Ow! – pull tiny hairs out of their foreheads," I explain. "Ow!"

She drops her hands and runs out of the room. Now I've – Ow! – gone and scared her.

I guess in time she'll discover all of the painful little truths about being a woman. The little uncomfortable things us girls endure day in and day out. Like hovering.

You know – hovering. It's what all proper girls do when they use a public restroom. It's painful.

And God help us if there isn't a lock on the stall. Then we have to hover, bend over and stretch our arm out what seems like a mile to hold the door shut. And, on occasion, if the hook's missing on the back of the broken door we have to hover, hold the door and our purse all at the same time so as not to let it touch the floor.

It makes your legs hurt.

I've tried explaining this to my husband. It's useless. I guess I can't expect a man who would rather go to the bathroom in the backyard than in his own house to understand.

Just the other night I locked him out and didn't know it. I had turned out the lights, locked up and was headed to turn on the security alarm when I heard a knock at the back door. I peeked through the window to see him standing there, rubbing his arms in the cold.

"What were you doing out there?" I asked after I'd let him in, but I knew the answer before it even came out of his mouth.

I cannot for the life of me understand why my husband would rather use the bathroom outdoors when there's perfectly good plumbing inside. It's like he's marking his territory or something.

"You've worked hard. You're a successful man who can afford not one, but four indoor toilets. Use them," I tell him. But he tells me that I just don't understand.

"I like it. It's a man thing," he says. "Besides, a lot of men do it."

I did not take much comfort in thinking that other men besides my own enjoy this. Instead, I found myself wondering if their wives found it just as baffling and, quite honestly, no-other-way-to-say-it... gross.

Besides the fact that he's probably killing my shrubbery, it's a potentially dangerous habit, I think. Wandering around in the back yard in the pitch black dark... he could get attacked by a dog, or even a squirrel. Then again, twelve men in the neighborhood out in the yard doing the same thing would probably come to his rescue.

I guess that's just one more painful little truth about being a woman – you're never going to change your man's habits. But should I remind him of the sticker bushes in the yard?

Nahhhh.

Ow!

Not quite back to normal

I stood looking at the doctor just the other day as she talked about what the next few weeks of our lives would be like. No bending. No stretching. No leaning over.

"Things aren't going to be back to normal for a while," she said.

We are at the hospital and it is the day following my husband's back surgery. For over a week my beloved had been unable to walk or sit, only lie flat on his back victim to a ruptured disc and no feeling in his left leg. But now, thanks to the good Lord and an awesome doctor, he was on the mend. We were going home.

I listened carefully to her instructions.

"That means no bending over to reach something on the floor, no throwing clothes in the dryer or picking up heavy laundry..."

Wait a minute. Had I in my tired stupor from trying to sleep on a hospital room chair wandered into the wrong room? I rubbed my eyes. Yes, still standing before me was the man I'd been married to for nearly 13 years, shaking his head with a somber determination like he was actually sad that he couldn't do laundry.

"Does he even know where the laundry room is?" I wanted to ask. But I kept quiet.

"No twisting... No driving for at least 10 days... No taking out the garbage..." his doctor continued.

Whoa. Back up. If he can't drive himself... who's going to....

"Do you realize how close you were to that car?"

It is 45 minutes later and we are checked out of the hospital and driving down Dawson Road. I am driving. My husband is buckled into the passenger's seat with a pained expression on his face.

"Honey, are you in pain?" I ask.

"No," he says. "You just can't drive. You're going to kill us."

He's grumpy. He's been through an agonizing week. He needs his pain medication. It makes him sleepy, doesn't it? Hmmmm. I press down harder on the gas to get to the pharmacy faster.

"When do you want this?" asks the clerk at the drive-thru window. "As soon as possible," I say sweetly, hoping she picks up on the pleading look on my face. I must have looked pitiful. She gave me a weak smile and told me it'd be 30 minutes. I look over at my husband and smile. I am so happy he's better.

"I'm taking you home now," I tell him and pull slowly out of the parking lot, careful to stay three car lengths from anyone in front of me.

The dogs welcome us in the driveway. I stay close to him on the steps and unlock the door. It's quiet inside.

"It's good to be home," he says, walking gingerly on his own two feet across the hallway and into the bedroom. Yes, it's good to be home and see the man I love feeling better again. I drop the overnight bag into a kitchen chair.

"It's going to be an interesting four to six weeks, wouldn't you say?" he yells from the back. "You and me. Here all day. Together."

Four to six weeks. At home. All day. Together.

Interesting? Most definitely.

If you need me, I'll be hiding in the laundry room.

Calling for back up

I ran to the driveway the other morning and plucked the newspaper from the bush beside the mailbox. It was cold. My bare feet were freezing.

"You went outside like that?" asked my son as I ran back into the house. "Did anybody see you?"

Oh, but to be a fly on the wall 20 years from now as he's telling his therapist about how his mom used to go outside in her pajamas, tell him she loves him in broad daylight, dance in the car and spit on her finger and clean his face.

"Yes, I went outside just like this," I said, modeling my full-length blue flannel pajama pants with matching long sleeved buttoned-to-the-collar top. "And your entire school rode by on the bus and saw me. Oh, and I danced in the driveway."

"Body armor," mumbled his dad, referring to my attire as he shuffled out of the kitchen with his coffee.

Later, after I'd safely deposited my children at the front of the school and my son had nearly broken his neck running into the building before I could roll down the window to yell "I love you," I settled on the sofa to fold laundry.

"Do you want to help?" I ask my husband, who has for the last three weeks been at home – the first with a bad back and the latter two recuperating from surgery.

"Oh, I don't think that would be good for my back," he moans. I know that's a fake pained expression. The whole time his eyes are glued to the television. Is he watching a special news bulletin? No. Is he watching a great movie? No. The local weather? No.

It's four women exercising on the beach, the waves crashing behind them.

"This looks really..." I begin. "Shhhh," he says. He shushes me, like any moment the exercising women are going to reveal something extraordinary, like the secret to obtaining world peace. A commercial comes on. He hates commercials. He starts channel surfing.

He settles on another program. A pilates exercise infomercial.

Three weeks ago, if you had asked my husband what pilates was he'd probably have said it was some kind of food.

"Look at that," he says to no one in particular. I concentrate on the contorted figure in spandex shorts with her legs flipped over her head sprawled across my television screen.

"I don't think that would be good for my back," I moan and fake a pained expression. He's not listening to me. I throw a balled up pair of socks at him.

"Shhhh," he says and throws them back. Apparently the pilates contorted woman will at any moment give us some life changing information, as well, and he doesn't want to miss it.

I wonder if he realizes an infomercial is just one big, long commercial? I guess it depends on how many clothes they're wearing.

I pick my pajamas out of my stack of laundry and fold them. They're still warm from the dryer. He might call them body armor, but at least I don't freeze like the women exercising on the beach wearing next to nothing obviously are. We're back to that channel, now.

"Don't you think they're freez…."

"Shhhhh," he says. There he goes shushing me again.

I bet if the exercising women asked him to help them fold the laundry, he'd do it. They could probably persuade him to put it up, too.

"Don't you want to help me put the laundry up?" I ask him.
There comes the fake pained expression again.

That's it. I'm calling in for back up. I just hope they can hear
me over the crashing waves.

Mandy Flynn

Light my fire

I walked outside just the other morning and the little hairs on my arms stood up. It was cold.

"Look, I can see my breath," said my daughter.

"As long as we can't smell it," said her brother.

Ahhh, the joys of winter.

I do love this season, burrowing under the covers like a chipmunk before the alarm goes off in the morning. Being the last one in bed and sticking my cold feet on my husband's back. A roaring fire in the fireplace.

A roaring fire. That's what I'll build on this cold morning right after I've dropped the kids off at school. I can hardly wait. A big fire. A warm drink. And my laptop.

If only our Labrador Retriever didn't smell, he could lay at my feet and the picture would be perfect.

Only... there is no wood. All that's left are wood crumbs. Our stack is gone.

To be entirely honest, it was two stacks. And, to make matters worse, they were just delivered the week of Christmas.

My husband has an addiction and it's name is firewood.

The head of our household fancies himself the King of All Firestarters. And I must admit, he's pretty darn good at it.

Only he can be obnoxious about it sometimes.

Seems he has this theory about firebuilding, where the wood has to be aligned and lit just so. It's a gift, he says. The alignment plus the proper timing of adding more firewood makes for the perfect blaze, he says.

If you have a death wish, you poke his fire when he's out of the room. He may not be able to find his socks on his own, but this man can spot an ember out of place from a mile away.

I first began to suspect he had a problem when he wanted to build a fire and it was nearly 70 degrees outside. Now we have an unwritten rule that it has to be at least below 60.

Like it is this morning. Only, I can't build a fire because we have no wood and I'm kind of embarrassed to call our wood supplier. This will be our fourth or fifth load since October. His name's Mr. Henry and, before long, he'll be able to retire to a tropical island with all the business we give him.

I tossed around ideas of what I could tell Mr. Henry so he wouldn't think we were crazy.

"We could tell him we gave a bunch of wood to our friends as Christmas gifts," I offered. "Or, we could tell him the dogs ate it."

My husband says I shouldn't be embarrassed, that we're probably some of his best customers. Still, we argued over who had to call him.

"We could buy wood at the grocery store," I offered.

The look I got told me that real men don't buy wood at the grocery store.

We called Mr. Henry and left him a message. Hopefully, he'll get back to us soon. I got new dining room chairs for Christmas and I caught my husband eyeing them.

"That's nice wood they're made of," he said. Did he just lick his lips?

That's it. I'm headed for the grocery store.

And if anybody asks me, the dogs ate all our firewood.

That's my story and I'm sticking to it.

Some days are made for worms

"You have to make sure it's a juicy one," she tells me, plunging her tiny hand into the blue, plastic cup. Knuckle deep in moist, chocolate brown soil she wiggles her fingers and offers up just what she's looking for.

"This one's juicy, all right," she proclaims as from between her dirt-caked thumb and

forefinger squirms a fat red wiggler. A worm.

"Is it a girl or a boy?" she asks, holding up her purple fishing pole as I weave the squirmy worm onto her hook.

"I really don't know," I confess. "Now, hold the pole really still or you're going to hook me."

"It's a rod, mommy. Not a pole," she corrects. Six-years-old and already an expert. "And I bet that worm's a girl cause she can wiggle. Like me."

Her pink flip-flop clad feet shuffle back and forth and she shakes her hips. The old, wooden dock creaks.

"Careful there wiggly girl," I tell her and grab hold of the leg of her jeans, afraid she might just topple over into the murky pond. A yellow ring of pollen clings to the muck at the edge of the bank where tadpoles play.

"I will throw it out myself," proclaims Miss Independent and I let go of her hook, worm in tow. I quickly cover my ears and face and lean over as far as I can get from the hook-wielding dancing girl. She pushes the button on her purple reel and flicks the whole thing forward, the orange bob plopping about five feet out.

"Nice job," I say, recovering from my protective crouch. "I know," she answers. Confidence. I like that. And then there was silence.

"Shhhhhh. Listen," I whisper. She kicks off her flip flops and sits down beside me.

"What are we shushing about?" she whispers back.

"Listen to the country," I whisper. "It makes you feel good."

She cocks her head sideways. The cool breeze picks up and swooshes through the pine trees overhead. She sidles up beside me, goose bumps on our arms.

Down the bank a ways her brother calls.

"Get the dog!" he yells. Bobbing above the tall, waving green grass I see our yellow lab leaping toward his fishing lure as it flashes in the sunlight, waiting to be cast. Unamused, the basset hound suns himself nearby.

We whistle. The dog turns his head to check us out and the sound of my 9-year-old's spinning reel fills the air. The proud defender of the fishing title, he's pulled in two good-sized bass already.

"Darn it!" says a little voice beside me.

My attention's brought back to the little fisherwoman, who's reeled in her hook only to find her worm gone, nibbled off most likely by the same naughty bream that's been teasing us all day.

"You want me to get you a worm?" I ask.

"No!" she says quickly. "I like to find the fat, juicy ones."

She takes off the pin pricked lid and grasps a handful of musty dirt, shaking it back and forth to uncover a ripe, fat victim. She holds him up and admires him in the sunlight. But something's wrong.

"We need to repaint my fingernails," she says matter-of-factly. "Pink."

Off in the distance her brother yells at the dog.

"That darn dog," she says as I wipe worm gunk onto the knees of my jeans and she poises for another cast. Whew! Near miss. I forgot to take cover.

We didn't catch any fish that afternoon. We did, however, catch the dog.

But he's just fine. And so are we.

Some days are just made for worms. We'll paint our nails tomorrow.

About the Author

Mandy Flynn was born and educated in rural Georgia as a true Southerner. A wife and mother of two, she draws from everyday experience to relate to her readers in a personal and touching voice.

The youngest daughter of six children, she began writing weekly columns at age 19 at the Americus Times Recorder, where she was recognized with Associated Press and Georgia Press Association awards. She and husband, Mike, have two children, son Trey, 10, and daughter Carter, 7. Mandy moved on to write for The Albany Herald in October 2003, where her column can be found each Sunday.

Printed in the United States
20510LVS00004BA/109-528

9 781418 440428